The Purpose of Jesus The Christ

Bible Studies, Volume 28

Leslie Rendell

Published by Leslie Rendell, 2024.

Introduction

The term "by the book" is given a whole new meaning in the life of Jesus Christ. There are hundreds of prophecies in the Bible that Jesus Christ fulfilled during his ministry here on earth. The Old Testament was written many years before the birth of Jesus Christ. Some of it was over one thousand years before his birth, yet Jesus managed to fulfil all the prophecies written about him. How could the men who wrote the books of the Old Testament possibly have known what they were writing would reflect the life story of one man? This is what I mean when I say Jesus lived his life "by the book."

Not only did Jesus fulfil these prophecies, but his life is also a fulfilment of the holy days of God. God gave Moses a list of sacred days the Israelites were to keep. It is amazing to discover that every major event in the life of our Lord occurred on one of these sacred days. As you read this book, I will describe how Jesus Christ fulfilled every one of these sacred days.

Listed below are the sacred days God commanded Moses to give to the people. You must understand one thing about this list of holy days. They are not the holy days of the Israelites, as many people believe today. Christians who keep these sacred days, and they are a minority of Christians, are accused of keeping "Jewish" holy days. But if you read this section of scripture carefully, you will see that these sacred days are God's. He has specifically said, "These are my appointed festivals, the appointed festivals of the LORD." He has given them for a particular reason, and I hope this will become evident to you as you read more of this book.

I will describe how Jesus Christ fulfilled every one of these holy days. You will see how the Bible is the recorded life of our Lord, written many years before Jesus was born. Moses led the people of Israel out of Egypt around 1447 BC. When the Israelites came out of Egypt, God gave them the holy days he required them, and us, to keep. These holy days are listed in the book of Leviticus. As you read through this list, understand that they are not the holy days of the Israelites, they are God's holy days.

Feasts of the Lord

Lev 23:1 The LORD said to Moses,

Lev 23:2 "Speak to the Israelites and say to them: 'These are my appointed festivals, the appointed festivals of the LORD, which you are to proclaim as sacred assemblies.

The Sabbath

Lev 23:3 "'There are six days when you may work, but the seventh day is a day of sabbath rest, a day of sacred assembly. You are not to do any work; wherever you live, it is a sabbath to the LORD.

The Passover

Lev 23:4 "'These are the LORD's appointed festivals, the sacred assemblies you are to proclaim at their appointed times:

Lev 23:5 The LORD's Passover begins at twilight on the fourteenth day of the first month.

Lev 23:6 On the fifteenth day of that month the LORD's Festival of Unleavened Bread begins; for seven days you must eat bread made without yeast.

Lev 23:7 On the first day hold a sacred assembly and do no regular work.

Lev 23:8 For seven days present a food offering to the LORD. And on the seventh day hold a sacred assembly and do no regular work.'"

The Feast of Firstfruits

Lev 23:9 The LORD said to Moses,

Lev 23:10 "Speak to the Israelites and say to them: 'When you enter the land I am going to give you and you reap its harvest, bring to the priest a sheaf of the first grain you harvest.

Lev 23:11 He is to wave the sheaf before the LORD so it will be accepted on your behalf; the priest is to wave it on the day after the Sabbath.

Lev 23:12 On the day you wave the sheaf, you must sacrifice as a burnt offering to the LORD a lamb a year old without defect,

Lev 23:13 together with its grain offering of two-tenths of an ephah of the finest flour mixed with olive oil—a food offering presented to the LORD, a pleasing aroma—and its drink offering of a quarter of a hin of wine.

Lev 23:14 You must not eat any bread, or roasted or new grain, until the very day you bring this offering to your God. This is to be a lasting ordinance for the generations to come, wherever you live.

The Feast of Weeks

Lev 23:15 "'From the day after the Sabbath, the day you brought the sheaf of the wave offering, count off seven full weeks.

Lev 23:16 Count off fifty days up to the day after the seventh Sabbath, and then present an offering of new grain to the LORD.

Lev 23:17 From wherever you live, bring two loaves made of two-tenths of an ephah of the finest flour, baked with yeast, as a wave offering of firstfruits to the LORD.

Lev 23:18 Present with this bread seven male lambs, each a year old and without defect, one young bull and two rams. They will be a burnt offering to the LORD, together with their grain offerings and drink offerings—a food offering, an aroma pleasing to the LORD.

Lev 23:19 Then sacrifice one male goat for a sin offering and two lambs, each a year old, for a fellowship offering.

Lev 23:20 The priest is to wave the two lambs before the LORD as a wave offering, together with the bread of the firstfruits. They are a sacred offering to the LORD for the priest.

Lev 23:21 On that same day you are to proclaim a sacred assembly and do no regular work. This is to be a lasting ordinance for the generations to come, wherever you live.

Lev 23:22 "'When you reap the harvest of your land, do not reap to the very edges of your field or gather the gleanings of your harvest. Leave them for the poor and for the foreigner residing among you. I am the LORD your God.'"

The Feast of Trumpets

Lev 23:23 The LORD said to Moses,

Lev 23:24 "Say to the Israelites: 'On the first day of the seventh month you are to have a day of sabbath rest, a sacred assembly commemorated with trumpet blasts.

Lev 23:25 Do no regular work, but present a food offering to the LORD.'"

The Day of Atonement

Lev 23:26 The LORD said to Moses,

Lev 23:27 "The tenth day of this seventh month is the Day of Atonement. Hold a sacred assembly and deny yourselves, and present a food offering to the LORD.

Lev 23:28 Do not do any work on that day, because it is the Day of Atonement, when atonement is made for you before the LORD your God.

Lev 23:29 Those who do not deny themselves on that day must be cut off from their people.

Lev 23:30 I will destroy from among their people anyone who does any work on that day.

Lev 23:31 You shall do no work at all. This is to be a lasting ordinance for the generations to come, wherever you live.

Lev 23:32 It is a day of sabbath rest for you, and you must deny yourselves. From the evening of the ninth day of the month until the following evening you are to observe your sabbath."

The Feast of Booths

Lev 23:33 The LORD said to Moses,

Lev 23:34 "Say to the Israelites: 'On the fifteenth day of the seventh month the LORD's Festival of Tabernacles begins, and it lasts for seven days.

Lev 23:35 The first day is a sacred assembly; do no regular work.

Lev 23:36 For seven days present food offerings to the LORD, and on the eighth day hold a sacred assembly and present a food offering to the LORD. It is the closing special assembly; do no regular work.

Lev 23:37 ("'These are the LORD's appointed festivals, which you are to proclaim as sacred assemblies for bringing food offerings to the LORD—the burnt offerings and grain offerings, sacrifices and drink offerings required for each day.

Lev 23:38 These offerings are in addition to those for the LORD's Sabbaths and in addition to your gifts and whatever you have vowed and all the freewill offerings you give to the LORD.)

Lev 23:39 "'So beginning with the fifteenth day of the seventh month, after you have gathered the crops of the land, celebrate the festival to the LORD for seven days; the first day is a day of sabbath rest, and the eighth day also is a day of sabbath rest.

Lev 23:40 On the first day you are to take branches from luxuriant trees—from palms, willows and other leafy trees—and rejoice before the LORD your God for seven days.

Lev 23:41 Celebrate this as a festival to the LORD for seven days each year. This is to be a lasting ordinance for the generations to come; celebrate it in the seventh month.

Lev 23:42 Live in temporary shelters for seven days: All native-born Israelites are to live in such shelters

Lev 23:43 so your descendants will know that I had the Israelites live in temporary shelters when I brought them out of Egypt. I am the LORD your God.'"

Lev 23:44 So Moses announced to the Israelites the appointed festivals of the LORD.

The Passover, the Feast of Unleavened Bread, the Feast of First Fruits, and the Feast of Weeks, also known as Pentecost, have all come to pass and all occurred in the springtime of the year. The other festivals have not yet been fulfilled, they are for a future time. Once you understand how exactly the springtime festivals have been fulfilled by our Lord, you should understand that the other festivals that will happen in the Autumn, are going to happen just as surely as the Springtime holy days occurred, and the meaning behind these holy days will also reflect a part of the life of Jesus Christ, and are a signpost to the future God has mapped out for us.

Mary And Joseph

The miracle surrounding the life of Jesus started even before he was born. Therefore, the story of Jesus must start with his parents. There is not a lot of biblical knowledge about them, but we will look at what has been recorded in the bible, and what we can deduce from the culture they were born into. The Israelites knew from the prophecies recorded in the Old Testament that their Messiah was due to arrive at about this time, and that a virgin would be the mother of their Messiah. This is recorded in the book of Isaiah that was written about 600 years before Jesus was born, recorded in Isa 7:14.

Isa 7:14 Therefore the Lord himself will give you a sign: The virgin will conceive and give birth to a son, and will call him Immanuel.

Mary, the mother of our Lord, was just like every other young woman who lived in the days Jesus was prophesied to be born. She planned to marry and have children and raise her family like all the other young women of the time. She was very devoted to her God, and she may have known that the promised messiah was due to come to Israel at about this time in history. But she could not have known beforehand that she was to be chosen to bring their Messiah into the world. She met Joseph and they were pledged to marry. There is no indication that she was to be the mother of our Lord until she was visited by the angel Gabriel, who gave her the news, as we see in Luk 1:26-35.

Luk 1:26 In the sixth month of Elizabeth's pregnancy, God sent the angel Gabriel to Nazareth, a town in Galilee,

Luk 1:27 to a virgin pledged to be married to a man named Joseph, a descendant of David. The virgin's name was Mary.

Luk 1:28 The angel went to her and said, "Greetings, you who are highly favored! The Lord is with you."

Luk 1:29 Mary was greatly troubled at his words and wondered what kind of greeting this might be.

Luk 1:30 But the angel said to her, "Do not be afraid, Mary; you have found favor with God.

Luk 1:31 You will conceive and give birth to a son, and you are to call him Jesus.

Luk 1:32 He will be great and will be called the Son of the Most High. The Lord God will give him the throne of his father David,

Luk 1:33 and he will reign over Jacob's descendants forever; his kingdom will never end."

Luk 1:34 "How will this be," Mary asked the angel, "since I am a virgin?"

Luk 1:35 The angel answered, "The Holy Spirit will come on you, and the power of the Most High will overshadow you. So the holy one to be born will be called the Son of God.

This part of Mary's life reveals to us that God chose her because she was highly favoured by God, as is clear from verse 28. She was a virgin and lived a life devoted to God and his laws. Therefore, God saw her as the perfect woman to carry his son. Verse 31 is the first time Mary knew she was to be the mother of Jesus. The news that she was to be the mother of our Lord must have been overwhelming for Mary, but she did not hesitate to accept that God had chosen her for this amazing task, as we see in Luk 1:38.

Luk 1:38 "I am the Lord's servant," Mary answered. "May your word to me be fulfilled." Then the angel left her.

Let's now examine how Joseph received the same information regarding the child Mary was carrying. He would have been shocked to learn that she was expecting, and he would have been extremely disappointed. The only thing Joseph could do as a law-abiding man was to file for divorce from her. However, the following scriptures from the book of Matthew also mention that he received a visit from a divine angel in Mat 1:18–25.

Mat 1:18 This is how the birth of Jesus the Messiah came about: His mother Mary was pledged to be married to Joseph, but before they came together, she was found to be pregnant through the Holy Spirit.

Mat 1:19 Because Joseph her husband was faithful to the law, and yet did not want to expose her to public disgrace, he had in mind to divorce her quietly.

Mat 1:20 But after he had considered this, an angel of the Lord appeared to him in a dream and said, "Joseph son of David, do not be afraid to take Mary home as your wife, because what is conceived in her is from the Holy Spirit.

Mat 1:21 She will give birth to a son, and you are to give him the name Jesus, because he will save his people from their sins."

Mat 1:22 All this took place to fulfill what the Lord had said through the prophet:

Mat 1:23 "The virgin will conceive and give birth to a son, and they will call him Immanuel" (which means "God with us").

Mat 1:24 When Joseph woke up, he did what the angel of the Lord had commanded him and took Mary home as his wife.

Mat 1:25 But he did not consummate their marriage until she gave birth to a son. And he gave him the name Jesus.

Now God advised Joseph in a dream about the child Mary was now carrying, and that the child was conceived by the Holy Spirit. This convinced Joseph to take Mary as his wife. This section of scripture also dispels the idea that Mary remained a virgin all her life. Read the last verse here, and you can see their marriage was not consummated until Jesus was born. Consummation is the first act of sexual intercourse between a husband and his wife. Their marriage was consummated after Jesus was born. After this, Joseph and Mary would have had a normal marriage, and that included having sex and having more children. The fact that Joseph and Mary had more children is exposed in Mat 13:54-56.

Mat 13:54 Coming to his hometown, he began teaching the people in their synagogue, and they were amazed. "Where did this man get this wisdom and these miraculous powers?" they asked.

Mat 13:55 "Isn't this the carpenter's son? Isn't his mother's name Mary, and aren't his brothers James, Joseph, Simon and Judas?

Mat 13:56 Aren't all his sisters with us? Where then did this man get all these things?"

Please remember that this is when Jesus visited his hometown of Nazareth, to teach about the Kingdom of God. The population of this small village where Jesus lived ranged between 480 and 1200. The figure is not exact, but it is close enough to indicate that everyone knew everyone in this small village. As a result, the residents were intimately familiar with Joseph and Mary, as well as their family. That is why they were able to name all of Jesus' brothers and knew he had sisters, as stated in the preceding verses.

Mary had already agreed to marry Joseph before being approached by the angel Gabriel. Until this point, she had no idea she would become our Lord's mother. She undoubtedly understood the Old Testament and was aware that the virgin birth would occur around this time in history. However, she had no way of knowing she was the virgin mentioned in Isa 7:14.

After Jesus' birth, Mary and Joseph would have had a normal marriage, with Joseph working as a carpenter and Mary running the household and caring for their children. They would have lived a very normal life after Jesus' birth until he began preaching about God's kingdom around the age of thirty.

Another thing to consider is that all of Jesus' siblings would have married and had their own children. These children would be Jesus' nieces and nephews. And from 2000 years ago, the members of Jesus' family would have numbered in the thousands. They were not Jesus' direct descendants because he never married or had his own children. Mary, the mother of Jesus, had at least one sister that is recorded in.

Joh 19:25 Near the cross of Jesus stood his mother, his mother's sister, Mary the wife of Clopas, and Mary Magdalene.

So Mary's sister would have been Jesus' Auntie. We do not know if Mary had any other siblings. So we have here a perfectly normal Jewish family in which Jesus grew up surrounded by numerous relatives.

The Birth Of Jesus

So now we'll look at the birth of Jesus and how it fulfilled other prophecies. We know Joseph and Mary lived in Nazareth; so why was Jesus born in Bethlehem? We can read about the reason for this in Luke.

Luk 2:1 In those days Caesar Augustus issued a decree that a census should be taken of the entire Roman world.

Luk 2:2 (This was the first census that took place while Quirinius was governor of Syria.)

Luk 2:3 And everyone went to their own town to register.

Luk 2:4 So Joseph also went up from the town of Nazareth in Galilee to Judea, to Bethlehem the town of David, because he belonged to the house and line of David.

Luk 2:5 He went there to register with Mary, who was pledged to be married to him and was expecting a child.

Luk 2:6 While they were there, the time came for the baby to be born,

Luk 2:7 and she gave birth to her firstborn, a son. She wrapped him in cloths and placed him in a manger, because there was no guest room available for them.

Therefore, Joseph had to go to Bethlehem to register for the census, and he had to take his very pregnant wife Mary with him. So now we must ask the question. "What is the significance of Jesus being born in Bethlehem instead of in his hometown of Nazareth?" The answer is intriguing and is a vital part of understanding the meaning of the life of Jesus Christ. We can see that it was prophesied that the Messiah was to be born in Bethlehem.

Mic 5:2 "But you, Bethlehem Ephrathah, though you are small among the clans of Judah, out of you will come for me one who will be ruler over Israel, whose origins are from of old, from ancient times."

Thus, when Jesus is born in Bethlehem, this prophecy is now realised. The Magi, or wise men from the east, are first mentioned in Matthew 2:1–6. They came seeking the one who would be crowned king of the Jews. Herod was not pleased with this news and wanted to know the birthplace of this new King.

Mat 2:1 After Jesus was born in Bethlehem in Judea, during the time of King Herod, Magi from the east came to Jerusalem

Mat 2:2 and asked, "Where is the one who has been born king of the Jews? We saw his star when it rose and have come to worship him."

Mat 2:3 When King Herod heard this he was disturbed, and all Jerusalem with him.

Mat 2:4 When he had called together all the people's chief priests and teachers of the law, he asked them where the Messiah was to be born.

Mat 2:5 "In Bethlehem in Judea," they replied, "for this is what the prophet has written:

Mat 2:6 "'But you, Bethlehem, in the land of Judah, are by no means least among the rulers of Judah; for out of you will come a ruler who will shepherd my people Israel.'"

Knowing that a new king had been born unsettled King Herod. He then called together his leading priests and legal experts to inquire about the expected birthplace of the Messiah. They informed him that the Messiah would be born in Bethlehem, as verse 5 above makes clear. The first indication that Herod had ill intentions was when he spoke to the Magi in secret. When Herod told the Magi he wished to go and worship this new King, he was lying.

Mat 2:7 Then Herod called the Magi secretly and found out from them the exact time the star had appeared.

Mat 2:8 He sent them to Bethlehem and said, "Go and search carefully for the child. As soon as you find him, report to me, so that I too may go and worship him."

Herod, however, had a secret agenda, and that was to have the Messiah, the new King, executed. This birth alarmed him, and he resolved to remove this fresh challenger to his throne in order to preserve his authority. For as long as there have been monarchs in human history, this has always been their scheme. Just take a look at the numerous individuals who were killed because they posed a threat to the ruling class of their era. Even in this supposedly modern day and age, it still occurs.

God protected the baby Jesus in two ways. First, he warned the Magi not to go and report their discovery to Herod, and then he warned Joseph in a dream to flee to Egypt to save his family from Herod.

Mat 2:12 And having been warned in a dream not to go back to Herod, they returned to their country by another route.

Mat 2:13 When they had gone, an angel of the Lord appeared to Joseph in a dream. "Get up," he said, "take the child and his mother and escape to Egypt. Stay there until I tell you, for Herod is going to search for the child to kill him."

Mat 2:14 So he got up, took the child and his mother during the night and left for Egypt,

Mat 2:15 where he stayed until the death of Herod. And so was fulfilled what the Lord had said through the prophet: "Out of Egypt I called my son."

This all proves that Jesus was born in Bethlehem. We know Joseph had to go there to register for the census, but what makes Bethlehem so important? Was it God's plan for Jesus to be born in that particular town, or did it just happen that way? As you read through this book, you will realise that God does not leave anything to chance, and that everything is part of His larger plan. Coincidences do not exist with God. So, why Bethlehem?

This is the area of Israel where the lambs to be slaughtered at the temple were born and raised. When John the Baptist saw Jesus approaching him for baptism, what did he call him? He called him the "Lamb of God."

Joh 1:29 The next day John saw Jesus coming toward him and said, "Look, the Lamb of God, who takes away the sin of the world!

Therefore, it is no coincidence that Jesus was born in Bethlehem. It was fitting that he was born there because he was the sacrificial lamb who died on the cross for the forgiveness of our sins. So being born in the same place as the temple lambs was appropriate.

But there is more to this than meets the eye. Bethlehem in the Aramaic language means "house of Bread". This also refers to the fact that Jesus called himself the "Bread of Life" in Joh 6:35. So Jesus being born to a virgin in Bethlehem at the correct time in history was all in God's plan. The same as the fact Bethlehem is the place where the sacrificial lambs are born, plus the fact Jesus calls himself the bread of life and was born in a village whose name means "house of Bread". These four facts are all supported in the bible.

Jesus was born in Bethlehem but his home was in Nazareth as is evident from the following passages of scripture. First in Mat 2:23.

Mat 2:23 and he went and lived in a town called Nazareth. So was fulfilled what was said through the prophets, that he would be called a Nazarene.

Jesus living in Nazareth is again emphasised when Mary Magdalene, Mary the mother of James, and Salome went to the tomb where Jesus had been laid out to anoint his body with the spices they had purchased. When they arrived at the tomb they were greeted by an angel as we see in.

Mar 16:5 As they entered the tomb, they saw a young man dressed in a white robe sitting on the right side, and they were alarmed.

Mar 16:6 "Don't be alarmed," he said. "You are looking for Jesus the Nazarene, who was crucified. He has risen! He is not here. See the place where they laid him.

The birth of Jesus is easy to verify from the bible. There is more evidence of the fact that Jesus was an actual person in history books other than the bible.

The Shepherds

The more you study the words of God the more you realise that God rarely chooses what is exalted and honoured in the world. God rather selects what is regarded by the world as lowly and insignificant to accomplish what he desires. This is the case with Bethlehem one of the smallest towns in Judah, yet from here Jesus would be born as a King.

Mic 5:2 But you, Bethlehem Ephrathah, being small among the clans of Judah, out of you one will come out to me that is to be ruler in Israel; whose goings out are from of old, from ancient times.

This prophecy from Micah was given hundreds of years before Jesus was born and is then retold in the new testament in Mat 2:6.

Mat 2:6 'You Bethlehem, land of Judah, are in no way least among the princes of Judah: for out of you shall come a governor, who shall shepherd my people, Israel.'"

One thing we can all take from this is the fact God can, and does, use the weakest things to accomplish his purposes. Therefore, none of us should ever consider we cannot be used by God in a great way. It does not matter what the world may think of you, it is only important what God thinks of you.

Two things we can learn from the following scriptures in the book of 1Samuel, is that David lived in Bethlehem and that he was a shepherd.

1Sa 16:1 The LORD said to Samuel, "How long will you mourn for Saul, since I have rejected him as king over Israel? Fill your horn with oil and be on your way; I am sending you to Jesse of Bethlehem. I have chosen one of his sons to be king."

Also.

1Sa 16:18 One of the servants answered, "I have seen a son of Jesse of Bethlehem who knows how to play the lyre. He is a brave man and a warrior. He speaks well and is a fine-looking man. And the LORD is with him."

1Sa 16:19 Then Saul sent messengers to Jesse and said, "Send me your son David, who is with the sheep."

So Jesus was born in the same place king David had lived years before. It is appropriate that David started his life as a shepherd because when Jesus arrived he was to be called a shepherd of his people.

Joh 10:9 I am the door. If anyone enters in by me, he will be saved, and will go in and go out, and will find pasture.

Joh 10:10 The thief only comes to steal, kill, and destroy. I came that they may have life, and may have it abundantly.

Joh 10:11 I am the good shepherd. The good shepherd lays down his life for the sheep.

As we see in Joh 10:11 Jesus is the good shepherd who was prepared to lay down his life for his sheep. We are his sheep and he certainly did lay down his life for us. He suffered death on the Roman cross so our sins could be forgiven. There has never been a greater act of love than this.

Shepherds played an important part in the birth of our Lord. They were the first to be told of the good news of his birth by the angel and they went to the place where he was born, and gave praise to their new born king as we see in Luk 2:8-12.

Luk 2:8 And there were shepherds living out in the fields nearby, keeping watch over their flocks at night.

Luk 2:9 An angel of the Lord appeared to them, and the glory of the Lord shone around them, and they were terrified.

Luk 2:10 But the angel said to them, "Do not be afraid. I bring you good news that will cause great joy for all the people.

Luk 2:11 Today in the town of David a Savior has been born to you; he is the Messiah, the Lord.

Luk 2:12 This will be a sign to you: You will find a baby wrapped in cloths and lying in a manger."

The shepherds were told by the angel where to find their newborn king, and it is important to consider the words the angel used when he told the shepherds how to recognise Jesus. He was to be in a manger and wrapped in cloths. The reason this is important is that no one would expect their king to be born in such humble circumstances, so they were forewarned so they could believe Jesus was their king because he fitted the description given to them by the angel. So the shepherds were prepared for what they were about to see, and they could embrace and believe in him even though he was born into such humble circumstances.

On What Day Was Jesus Crucified

When it comes to what happened on the day Jesus was crucified, there is a lot of information recorded for us in the bible. Some of this information is indisputable and is very clear. Unfortunately, some aspects of this day are controversial and therefore need a careful study of the scriptures to ascertain what is correct and what is false.

The time Jesus was crucified, the time of his death on the cross, and the time he was placed in the tomb are all facts that cannot be disputed. These aspects of our Lord's death cannot be denied, so what is controversial about this event?

The majority of traditional churches teach that Jesus died on "Good Friday" and rose from the dead on "Easter Sunday". But what is the evidence that we can get from studying the Bible? Is there sufficient proof in the scriptures to dispute these claims, even though as I stated earlier they are what the majority of traditional churches teach? I believe there is more than enough evidence to disprove the "Good Friday", and "Easter Sunday" traditions. To do this, will require the reader to honestly seek the truth. If you refuse to accept what the bible is telling you, then you will never see the truth. You need to let go of man's traditions and listen to the word of God.

The truth is in the bible, but you will not find it neatly wrapped up in one place. Please consider the meaning of the following scripture.

Pro 25:2 It is the glory of God to conceal a thing: but the honour of kings is to search out a matter.

So God has concealed things in his bible and he expects us to search for them as is made even more clear in Isa 28:10.

Isa 28:10 For it is precept on precept, precept on precept; line on line, line on line; here a little, there a little.

From these passages of scripture, we can see God expects us to do our diligent research and look for what he has concealed for us to find. If you do not do this, but just rely on what you are told by any human, then you will never get to the truth on this or any other matter in the Bible. Whether you commit to the study of the Bible or not is your concern. I guess it all comes down to just how important the truth is to you.

I have found the best way to come to terms with the correct day Jesus was crucified is to follow the activities of the women from the time Jesus was crucified until the time he was resurrected from the tomb. Women at the time of Jesus were regarded as lower-class citizens. Their testimony in a court of law was regarded as unreliable. Women are still thought of this way in many countries around the world, especially in the Middle East.

Christians know better than this, or at least they should, because God explains to us that we are all equal. He makes this clear in Gal 3:28.

Gal 3:28 There is neither Jew nor Gentile, neither slave nor free, nor is there male and female, for you are all one in Christ Jesus.

I believe God allows us to find the truth through the amazing women who followed Jesus and supported him in his ministry. In this way, he is also letting us know how much he appreciated them at that time and how he still does in this modern day and age.

The first part of uncovering what God has concealed is in the following scriptures that describe the time Jesus died on the cross until he was taken down and placed in the tomb. Remember, we are looking to see what the women were doing during the days of Christ's crucifixion until his resurrection from the dead.

Luk 23:46 Jesus called out with a loud voice, "Father, into your hands I commit my spirit." When he had said this, he breathed his last.

Luk 23:47 The centurion, seeing what had happened, praised God and said, "Surely this was a righteous man."

Luk 23:48 When all the people who had gathered to witness this sight saw what took place, they beat their breasts and went away.

Luk 23:49 But all those who knew him, including the women who had followed him from Galilee, stood at a distance, watching these things.

Luk 23:50 Now there was a man named Joseph, a member of the Council, a good and upright man,

Luk 23:51 who had not consented to their decision and action. He came from the Judean town of Arimathea, and he himself was waiting for the kingdom of God.

Luk 23:52 Going to Pilate, he asked for Jesus' body.

Luk 23:53 Then he took it down, wrapped it in linen cloth and placed it in a tomb cut in the rock, one in which no one had yet been laid.

Luk 23:54 It was Preparation Day, and the Sabbath was about to begin.

Luk 23:55 The women who had come with Jesus from Galilee followed Joseph and saw the tomb and how his body was laid in it.

Luk 23:56 Then they went home and prepared spices and perfumes. But they rested on the Sabbath in obedience to the commandment.

Let us now examine these verses and uncover what they are telling us. In verse 47 we have the witness of the Centurion Guard who was there to witness the entire event. He had no doubt seen many criminals crucified, but there was something different about the crucifixion of Jesus, so much so that the Centurion was compelled to say. "Surely this was a righteous man". He would have seen the rocks split, felt to ground shake, and maybe even seen the tombs open.

In verse 48 the people who had followed the event of the crucifixion hoping to see Jesus defeat death on the cross were now disappointed. It was now close to the start of the Sabbath so they returned to their homes.

One important verse to consider is verse 49. Please notice that all those who knew him, not just those who were there to see the entertainment, but those who actually knew Jesus. His friends and family and most importantly all of the women were there.

Verse 50 introduces us to Joseph of Arimathaea who went to Pilot to request the body of Jesus so he could be buried. When he was given permission he wrapped the body of Jesus in linen and placed it in the tomb. This all happened on the preparation day as the Sabbath was about to begin as we see in verse 54.

Verse 55 is also very important if we are to fully understand what occurred that day. The women all saw the body of Jesus put into the tomb and how his body was laid out in the tomb. And this happened as the Sabbath was about to begin.

In verse 56 we are told the women went home and prepared the spices to anoint the body of Jesus. The way this reads it appears this all happened on the same day Jesus was crucified. On the preparation day for the Sabbath. But which Sabbath are we talking about?

To decide what Sabbath this is referring to, we must remember on what day the crucifixion took place. It was on the day of the Passover which always falls on the 14th of Nisan. This is always followed by the "Feast of Unleavened Bread" on the 15th of Nisan, and the first day of this feast is always regarded by God as a Sabbath day. Check out the scriptures in Lev 23:4-7.

Lev 23:4 "'These are the LORD's appointed festivals, the sacred assemblies you are to proclaim at their appointed times:

Lev 23:5 The LORD's Passover begins at twilight on the fourteenth day of the first month.

Lev 23:6 On the fifteenth day of that month the LORD's Festival of Unleavened Bread begins; for seven days you must eat bread made without yeast.

Lev 23:7 On the first day hold a sacred assembly and do no regular work.

Therefore the Sabbath that was about to begin was not a usual Saturday Sabbath. No, it was the Sabbath for the first day of unleavened bread as the above scriptures from Lev 23:4-7 prove.

Now, one of the most vital verses to understand is Mar 16:1. Remember, according to Pro 25:2, God has concealed things and in Isa 28:10 we must search Precept upon precept, line upon line, here a little there a little. So now read Mar 16:1 and place this event in the timeline of events.

Mar 16:1 And when the sabbath was past, Mary Magdalene, and Mary the mother of James, and Salome, had bought sweet spices, that they might come and anoint him.

Now we can see the women waited until the Sabbath of the 15th of Nisan was over, the first day of the feast of unleavened bread, before they went and purchased the spices. The reason for them waiting for the Sabbath to be over was because when they were at the tomb watching Jesus being laid out, it was as the Sabbath was about to begin and they did not have sufficient time to purchase the necessary spices before the Sabbath started. So to keep the Sabbath day law of doing no physical work on the day, they rested.

Plus any storekeeper selling the spices would have closed shop well before sunset to also be compliant with the Sabbath day laws. So the women could not possibly purchase the spices on the day of preparation the day Jesus was crucified.

So the women rested on the Sabbath which was the first day of Unleavened Bread as we are told in Mar 16:1. Then they purchased and prepared the spices, then rested on the Sabbath. This Sabbath day was the normal weekly Sabbath, so now we can plainly see 2 Sabbaths with one normal day in between them. Therefore, the spices were purchased and prepared on this day between the 2 Sabbath days, and since the second Sabbath was the weekly Sabbath, the spices must have been purchased and prepared on Friday two days after Jesus was crucified on a Wednesday.

In the following chapter "The Sign Of Jonah" we will establish that Jesus was to be in the tomb for exactly 72 hours. If he was to prove he is the Son Of God, then he had to be in the tomb for that exact amount of time. We also know he was put into the tomb as the "Special Sabbath" on the first day of the feast of unleavened bread was about to begin. This means very late in the day as the sun was about to set.

Therefore, since Jesus was to be in the tomb for exactly 72 hours, he had to rise from the dead 72 hours after he was laid out in the tomb. This means he had to be resurrected from the dead at the same time of the day he was laid out in the tomb, just before sunset three days and three nights later. Anything else, and he is a false Messiah.

We have also seen the women purchase and prepare the spices on the day before the weekly Sabbath. They then rested on the Sabbath according to the Sabbath laws. We learn from this the women could not go to the tomb before the weekly Sabbath was over, so let us continue the story from Luk 24:1-3.

Luk 24:1 Now upon the first day of the week, very early in the morning, they came unto the sepulchre, bringing the spices which they had prepared, and certain others with them.

Luk 24:2 And they found the stone rolled away from the sepulchre.

Luk 24:3 And they entered in, and found not the body of the Lord Jesus.

The women went to the tomb very early on the first day of the week, and found the stone rolled back, and the tomb was empty. Therefore, Jesus had already risen from the tomb before the women arrived, very early in the first day of the week, Sunday.

We know at what time of the day Jesus had to rise from the tomb, and that is just as the sun was setting, so if he was not there very early on the first day of the week, then the only explanation is that he was resurrected the day before, on the weekly Sabbath.

I stated earlier that Jesus was crucified, died, and was put into the tomb on a Wednesday. So now to prove that point from a different perspective. We now know when Jesus rose from the dead, so to establish the day Jesus was crucified, let us count back 72 hours from just before sunset on the Sabbath, and you will arrive just before sunset on Wednesday.

Following this time frame, we can see it fits exactly into the three days and three nights of prophecy Jesus gave the Jewish leaders when they were asking him for a sign about his death and resurrection. It is also important to recall that this was the only sign he was going to give them.

Also note how the other expressions "in three days," "after three days," and "on the third day" all fit perfectly into this timetable.

Jesus performed many miracles during his ministry here on earth, yet the Pharisees still refused to believe he was their Messiah. So Jesus fulfilled the only sign he was going to give them to prove he was who he claimed to be. This one sign, three days and three nights, or the sign of Jonah, proves to us all that Jesus Christ is the Messiah of the Jews and our Messiah as well.

The proof is all there, it is a shame people cannot see it, and in many cases, they just refuse to see it because it does not fit neatly into what they already believe. The man-made traditions of "Good Friday" and "Easter Sunday" have proven to be wrong if you are going to put the word of God before the words and traditions of man. Who are you going to believe?

There is a great deal of information concealed in the Bible. Things we can easily read over and not see the reason for the information to be in the Bible. One of the passages of scripture that is important for us to fully understand is recorded in Joh 19:31–34.

Joh 19:31 Therefore the Jews, because it was the Preparation Day, so that the bodies wouldn't remain on the cross on the Sabbath (for that Sabbath was a special one), asked of Pilate that their legs might be broken, and that they might be taken away.

Joh 19:32 Therefore the soldiers came, and broke the legs of the first, and of the other who was crucified with him;

Joh 19:33 but when they came to Jesus, and saw that he was already dead, they didn't break his legs.

Joh 19:34 However one of the soldiers pierced his side with a spear, and immediately blood and water came out.

Jesus was crucified on a Roman cross, and before this he was scourged with a whip called a falgrum. It was a vicious and cruel instrument of torture for anyone about to be crucified. This whip was made from braided leather with metal balls and sharp pieces of bone interwoven into the leather. The metal balls were to add weight to the whip to cause deep bruising to the victim. The sharp bones cut into the flesh resulting in cuts to the muscles, underlying veins and would even expose the bowels.

Jesus would have suffered from hypovolemic shock, or low blood pressure caused by the loss of so much blood. This would have caused the heart to beat quickly to try to pump blood that was not available, and he suffered from extreme thirst as his body wanted to replenish the lost fluids his beating has resulted in.

As Jesus carried his cross to Golgotha he collapsed due to this low blood pressure. As Jesus hung on the cross he said he was thirsty, this is another symptom of low blood pressure.

This hypovolemic shock would also cause fluid to gather in the sacks that surround the heart and lungs. This is the reason why when the Roman guard thrust his spear into Jesus, blood and water came out of his wound as recorded in Joh 19:34 above.

Most people do not realise the punishment Jesus went through when he was crucified. From the above description of a Roman flogging you can see he would have been severely disfigured, read the following from the Old Testament, this is a prophecy about Jesus and the torture he was to undergo. Read especially verse 14.

Isa 52:13 See, my servant will act wisely; he will be raised and lifted up and highly exalted.

Isa 52:14 Just as there were many who were appalled at him— his appearance was so disfigured beyond that of any human being and his form marred beyond human likeness—

Isa 52:15 so he will sprinkle many nations, and kings will shut their mouths because of him. For what they were not told, they will see, and what they have not heard, they will understand.

Jesus was not just hung on a cross, he was whipped beyond recognition before he was taken to Golgotha. He survived approximately six hours on the cross and would have suffered immense pain.

This is what our Saviour did for you and me. So when you think of him on that Roman cross, remember what he suffered.

The sign of Jonah

One very important piece of evidence that is almost always interpreted incorrectly is the term Jesus used to describe the amount of time he was going to be in the tomb. Let us start looking at this in the book of Matthew.

Mat 12:38 Then some of the Pharisees and teachers of the law said to him, "Teacher, we want to see a sign from you."

Mat 12:39 He answered, "A wicked and adulterous generation asks for a sign! But none will be given it except the sign of the prophet Jonah.

Mat 12:40 For as Jonah was three days and three nights in the belly of a huge fish, so the Son of Man will be three days and three nights in the heart of the earth.

There are two things that you need to understand here. First, Jesus told the Pharisees that he was going to give them only one sign that he was who he claimed to be. This is the sign of the prophet Jonah. This is the only sign he was going to use; therefore, it is vital that we get this right. Jesus expounded on what he meant by the term "the sign of Jonah" when he added, "The son of man will be three days and three nights in the heart of the earth."

Since this is the only sign, Jesus had to fulfil it perfectly, otherwise he is an impostor and not the Son of God. It is also essential that we understand exactly what this term means and not twist the words to mean what we want them to mean. But this is what many people have done to make the term "three days and three nights" fit into their private thoughts on the matter. In reality, the only interpretation that we should consider is according to the scriptures. We know Jesus died for our sins according to the scriptures in 1Co 15:3-4.

1Co 15:3 For I delivered unto you first of all that which I also received, how that Christ died for our sins according to the scriptures;

1Co 15:4 And that he was buried, and that he rose again the third day according to the scriptures:

So now that we know Jesus died for our sins according to the scriptures, let us see what the scriptures say. The thoughts and traditions of man should never enter the calculations for the time Jesus was in the tomb. We can only rely on the Bible for accurate information.

Where can we go in the Bible to find this information? The very first book in the Bible starts with Genesis 1:1. We need to read from here to Genesis 1:13. This describes the first three days of creation, covering three nights and three days. This can only mean a total of 72 hours, as there are three periods of night and three periods of day, each with 12 hours.

The Bible uses other terms as well, so we can pinpoint the time to exactly 72 hours. Not an hour more or an hour less. In the following scriptures, we see the term "the third day" used to describe when He would be raised from the dead.

Mat 20:17 And Jesus going up to Jerusalem took the twelve disciples apart in the way, and said unto them,

Mat 20:18 Behold, we go up to Jerusalem; and the Son of man shall be betrayed unto the chief priests and unto the scribes, and they shall condemn him to death,

Mat 20:19 And shall deliver him to the Gentiles to mock, and to scourge, and to crucify him: and the third day he shall rise again.

This term is used again in Luk 24:46.

Luk 24:46 And said unto them, Thus it is written, and thus it behoved Christ to suffer, and to rise from the dead the third day.

Therefore, Jesus rose from the dead on the third day. The Bible then uses the term in three days in thc book of John.

Joh 2:19 Jesus answered and said unto them, Destroy this temple, and in three days I will raise it up.

Joh 2:20 Then said the Jews, Forty and six years was this temple in building, and wilt thou rear it up in three days?

Joh 2:21 But he spake of the temple of his body.

Next, we are told he would be raised **after three days.**

Mar 8:31 He began to teach them that the Son of Man must suffer many things, and be rejected by the elders, the chief priests, and the scribes, and be killed, and after three days rise again.

The book of Matthew also records this term in.

Mat 27:63 Saying, Sir, we remember that that deceiver said, while he was yet alive, After three days I will rise again.

These three terms will furthermore pinpoint the exact time for us to 72 hours. First, we have the term "the third day" meaning three days after they buried him. This time frame is explained in Gen 1:1 to Gen 1:13 and can only mean 72 hours. Then we see the term "in three days" and this means inside three days, or no longer than three days or 72 hours. And finally, we have the term "after three days", no less than three days, it must be a full 72 hours but no longer. These terms confirm Jesus was in the tomb for the full three days and three nights, or more precisely, 72 hours.

Passover

What is the sequence of events for the first Passover, when the Israelites were preparing to leave Egypt? The order of these events must be a guide for us today as we celebrate the Passover. Therefore, it is vital that we start at the very beginning, something very few people do. Every part of the Passover is critical to understand if you want the full and correct interpretation of these days.

In the book of Exodus we have the story of the original exodus from Egypt. So, let us start our research here by reading Exo 12:1-6 and understand the correct sequence of events.

Exo 12:1 The LORD said to Moses and Aaron in Egypt,

Exo 12:2 "This month is to be for you the first month, the first month of your year.

Exo 12:3 Tell the whole community of Israel that on the tenth day of this month each man is to take a lamb for his family, one for each household.

Exo 12:4 If any household is too small for a whole lamb, they must share one with their nearest neighbor, having taken into account the number of people there are. You are to determine the amount of lamb needed in accordance with what each person will eat.

Exo 12:5 The animals you choose must be year-old males without defect, and you may take them from the sheep or the goats.

Exo 12:6 Take care of them until the fourteenth day of the month, when all the members of the community of Israel must slaughter them at twilight.

In verse two God tells Moses and Aaron that this is to be the first month of the year for them. It is Aviv, also known as Nisan. I will call this month Nisan in this book, but remember it is also called Aviv.

When we consider the Passover in this modern day and age, we generally do not start at the very beginning. So let us rectify that here and start our research in verse 3. This happens on the 10th day of Nisan. On this day, the Israelites were to select a lamb without defect and take it into their homes until the 14th of Nisan. Some points to keep in mind from this section of scripture are.

1. This all happens in the first month of the year, the month of Nisan which occurs in the springtime.

2. The animals to be chosen are to be one year old and without defects. One thing to remember here is these lambs were to be one year old. This means they had to be born at about this same time of the year exactly one year earlier. This fact will become more important later in this book.

3. These lambs were to be taken into their homes and cared for until the 14th of Nisan.

4. The lambs were to be slaughtered at twilight on the 14th of Nisan. There is a lot of confusion about when the lambs were to be slaughtered. You would think that from the instructions God has given to the Israelites here, that the time should be indisputable. But this time varies from a different understanding of these simple instructions from God. The time varies from early on the 14th of Nisan to late on the 14th of Nisan. This all comes about by not understanding the correct meaning of "at twilight on the 14th".

So how can we properly understand what this means? First, we must remember that the Jewish days always start and finish at sunset, not at midnight as is the custom of the Western world. Now there can only be one twilight period each day, so when is twilight on the 14th of Nisan? Twilight refers to the time of the day when the sun has set and just before full darkness sets in. Therefore, twilight on the 14th of Nisan was immediately after the sun had set and the 14th had only just started. This is the time for the slaughtering of the lambs, at the very start of the day when the day is just one, or maybe two hours old.

Some claim that this twilight, when the lambs are to be slaughtered, is at the end of the 14th. The trouble with that interpretation is that the twilight at the end of the 14th is actually at the start of the 15th of Nisan, and God has very clearly stated that the lambs were to be slaughtered on the 14th, not the 15th.

These events that occurred before the 14th will become important to remember later in this book, so I hope you have understood what Exo 12:1-6 is revealing to you.

Also remember that the 14th of Nisan is not a holy day. It is always referred to as "preparation day." Preparing for the Sabbath, which is the first day of the feast of unleavened bread. The first holy day is on the 15th of Nisan because this is the first day of the feast of unleavened bread.

Palm Saturday

I have covered the fact that Jesus Christ was crucified on a Wednesday, not on a Friday, as traditional Christianity will teach you. I covered this in the chapter titled "On What Day Was Jesus Crucified". Therefore, the "Good Friday" and "Easter Sunday" concepts are false and misleading. So now I must ask. What other aspects of the "Easter" tradition has secular Christianity failed to understand correctly? The purpose of this chapter is to answer the question. Did Jesus enter Jerusalem on the donkey on Sunday as is also taught by traditional Christianity? If they got the "Good Friday", and "Easter Sunday" wrong, then the chance of them also getting the day Jesus entered Jerusalem wrong is also a very high probability.

In this chapter of the book, I will endeavour to prove to you that Jesus entered Jerusalem on a donkey on a Saturday, not on a Sunday.

To prove this point we must go back to the very first Passover, the day before the Israelites left Egypt. We must establish the order of things about the Passover. Most people when they are discussing the Passover start with the 14th day of Nisan because this is the day Jesus was crucified, many even get this day wrong even though it is very plainly stated in the bible that the Passover is on a preparation day that is the 14th of Nisan. But to get the full story we must go back four more days to the 10th of Nisan. Consider the following passage of scripture from the book of Exodus as we find in the "World English Bible"

Exo 12:1 Yahweh spoke to Moses and Aaron in the land of Egypt, saying,

Exo 12:2 "This month shall be to you the beginning of months. It shall be the first month of the year to you.

Exo 12:3 Speak to all the congregation of Israel, saying, 'On the tenth day of this month, they shall take to them every man a lamb, according to their fathers' houses, a lamb for a household;

Exo 12:4 and if the household is too little for a lamb, then he and his neighbor next to his house shall take one according to the number of the souls; according to what everyone can eat you shall make your count for the lamb.

Exo 12:5 Your lamb shall be without defect, a male a year old. You shall take it from the sheep, or from the goats:

Exo 12:6 and you shall keep it until the fourteenth day of the same month; and the whole assembly of the congregation of Israel shall kill it at evening.

On the 10th of Nisan, the Israelites were told to select a one-year-old lamb without blemish and bring it into their homes. They were to keep this lamb in the house until the 14th of Nisan and then slaughter it at twilight. The blood of the lamb was then to be painted on the door frames of their homes and this would cause the death angel to "Passover" them, and not kill the first-born of the Israelites in these houses.

Those two dates, the 10th and the 14th of Nisan are very important to keep in mind.

Jesus fulfilled all the holy days God ordained the Israelites to keep in the springtime of the year. The holy days in the Autumn months are yet to be fulfilled at the close of this age. He was crucified on the 14th of Nisan and the waving of the sheaf of the "Firstfruits" represented the ascension of Jesus after he rose from the dead on the Sabbath and ascended the day after the Sabbath. This is covered in the chapter "The First Fruits" We see the original command to wave the sheaf of firstfruits the day after the Sabbath in Lev 23:9-11.

Lev 23:9 Yahweh spoke to Moses, saying,

Lev 23:10 "Speak to the children of Israel, and tell them, 'When you have come into the land which I give to you, and shall reap its harvest, then you shall bring the sheaf of the first fruits of your harvest to the priest:

Lev 23:11 and he shall wave the sheaf before Yahweh, to be accepted for you. On the next day after the Sabbath the priest shall wave it.

The fact that Jesus ascended to heaven on the first day of the week, Sunday is further explained in the chapter "The Thief On The Cross".

The day Jesus entered Jerusalem and the palm branches were spread out before him is fulfilling the 10th of Nisan when the sacrificial lambs were selected and brought into the homes. On the 10th of Nisan, four days before he was crucified he came to his father's house, the temple as the selected lamb to be sacrificed where his blood would cover the sins of all people of all ages.

We have established the Passover was on Wednesday the 14th of Nisan, so if we count backward the four days to when the sacrificial lamb was selected, what day do we come to?

Wednesday the 14th. Passover and the day Jesus was crucified

Day one. Tuesday the 13th of Nisan

Day two. Monday the 12th of Nisan

Day three. Sunday the 11th of Nisan

Day four. Saturday the 10th of Nisan,

The day the sacrificial lamb was selected was on the 10th of Nisan. We are made aware of this in Exo 10:3. The day Jesus entered Jerusalem on the donkey and presented himself in his Father's house, the temple was also on the 10th of Nisan.

From this evidence alone we should accept Jesus rode into Jerusalem on the donkey on Palm Saturday, and not on Palm Sunday.

But we are going to need more proof than this, and the only place we can find it is in the Bible. No other "authority" should be accepted on such an important matter as this. The traditions of man are especially misleading and must not be considered if you are truly seeking the truth on this all-important matter. This is why I will rely only on what is evident from the bible.

There are a lot of scriptures following, but this is necessary to prove what I am claiming. The 10th of Nisan was the day Jesus entered Bethlehem.

When this happened Jesus was fulfilling the meaning of the day the Israelites selected their lambs ready for them to be sacrificed four days later. The lambs were brought into the father's house as the lambs to be sacrificed. Jesus came to his Father's house, the temple, to offer himself as the lamb to be sacrificed for the forgiveness of the sins of all people. This all happened on the 10th of Nisan. Therefore the events from Mar 11:1 to Mar 11:11 cover this day.

Mar 11:1 When they came near to Jerusalem, to Bethsphage and Bethany, at the Mount of Olives, he sent two of his disciples,

Mar 11:2 and said to them, "Go your way into the village that is opposite you. Immediately as you enter into it, you will find a young donkey tied, on which no one has sat. Untie him, and bring him.

Mar 11:3 If anyone asks you, 'Why are you doing this?' say, 'The Lord needs him;' and immediately he will send him back here."

Mar 11:4 They went away, and found a young donkey tied at the door outside in the open street, and they untied him.

Mar 11:5 Some of those who stood there asked them, "What are you doing, untying the young donkey?"

Mar 11:6 They said to them just as Jesus had said, and they let them go.

Mar 11:7 They brought the young donkey to Jesus, and threw their garments on it, and Jesus sat on it.

Mar 11:8 Many spread their garments on the way, and others were cutting down branches from the trees, and spreading them on the road.

Mar 11:9 Those who went in front, and those who followed, cried out, "Hosanna! Blessed is he who comes in the name of the Lord!

Mar 11:10 Blessed is the kingdom of our father David that is coming in the name of the Lord! Hosanna in the highest!"

Mar 11:11 Jesus entered into the temple in Jerusalem. When he had looked around at everything, it being now evening, he went out to Bethany with the twelve.

This is where the 10th of Nisan ends. What we must look for now is when a new day begins after Jesus has ridden into Jerusalem, and follow the events day by day until we come to the Passover. In Mar 11:12 we see the start of the next day, this is the 11th of Nisan.

Mar 11:12 The next day, (Author's comment - the 11th of Nisan) when they had come out from Bethany, he was hungry.

Mar 11:13 Seeing a fig tree afar off having leaves, he came to see if perhaps he might find anything on it. When he came to it, he found nothing but leaves, for it was not the season for figs.

Mar 11:14 Jesus told it, "May no one ever eat fruit from you again!" and his disciples heard it.

Mar 11:15 They came to Jerusalem, and Jesus entered into the temple, and began to throw out those who sold and those who bought in the temple, and overthrew the money changers' tables, and the seats of those who sold the doves.

Mar 11:16 He would not allow anyone to carry a container through the temple.

Mar 11:17 He taught, saying to them, "Isn't it written, 'My house will be called a house of prayer for all the nations?' But you have made it a den of robbers!"

Mar 11:18 The chief priests and the scribes heard it, and sought how they might destroy him. For they feared him, because all the multitude was astonished at his teaching.

Mar 11:19 When evening came, he went out of the city.

Jesus and his disciples went back to Bethany and stayed there that night. Now continuing in verse 20 we see the start of the next day, and this will be the 12th of Nisan, From here we must count the days until the Passover and see if the days correspond with the timing of the original Passover that Jesus came to fulfil.

From Mar 11:20 till the end of chapter 13, a lot happened. Jesus had a very busy day but there is no indication of this day ending or another day starting. So all this happened on the 12th of Nisan. Please read through this section of scripture and settle in your own minds that this day continues until we come to Mar 14:1.

Mar 11:20 As they passed by in the morning, (Author's comment - the 12th of Nisan) they saw the fig tree withered away from the roots.

Mar 11:21 Peter, remembering, said to him, "Rabbi, look! The fig tree which you cursed has withered away."

Mar 11:22 Jesus answered them, "Have faith in God.

Mar 11:23 For most certainly I tell you, whoever may tell this mountain, 'Be taken up and cast into the sea,' and doesn't doubt in his heart, but believes that what he says is happening; he shall have whatever he says.

Mar 11:24 Therefore I tell you, all things whatever you pray and ask for, believe that you have received them, and you shall have them.

Mar 11:25 Whenever you stand praying, forgive, if you have anything against anyone; so that your Father, who is in heaven, may also forgive you your transgressions.

Mar 11:26 But if you do not forgive, neither will your Father in heaven forgive your transgressions."

Mar 11:27 They came again to Jerusalem, and as he was walking in the temple, the chief priests, and the scribes, and the elders came to him,

Mar 11:28 and they began saying to him, "By what authority do you do these things? Or who gave you this authority to do these things?"

Mar 11:29 Jesus said to them, "I will ask you one question. Answer me, and I will tell you by what authority I do these things.

Mar 11:30 The baptism of John—was it from heaven, or from men? Answer me."

Mar 11:31 They reasoned with themselves, saying, "If we should say, 'From heaven;' he will say, 'Why then did you not believe him?'

Mar 11:32 If we should say, 'From men'"—they feared the people, for all held John to really be a prophet.

Mar 12:1 He began to speak to them in parables. "A man planted a vineyard, put a hedge around it, dug a pit for the wine press, built a tower, rented it out to a farmer, and went into another country.

Mar 12:2 When it was time, he sent a servant to the farmer to get from the farmer his share of the fruit of the vineyard.

Mar 12:3 They took him, beat him, and sent him away empty.

Mar 12:4 Again, he sent another servant to them; and they threw stones at him, wounded him in the head, and sent him away shamefully treated.

Mar 12:5 Again he sent another; and they killed him; and many others, beating some, and killing some.

Mar 12:6 Therefore still having one, his beloved son, he sent him last to them, saying, 'They will respect my son.'

Mar 12:7 But those farmers said among themselves, 'This is the heir. Come, let's kill him, and the inheritance will be ours.'

Mar 12:8 They took him, killed him, and cast him out of the vineyard.

Mar 12:9 What therefore will the lord of the vineyard do? He will come and destroy the farmers, and will give the vineyard to others.

Mar 12:10 Haven't you even read this Scripture: 'The stone which the builders rejected, the same was made the head of the corner.

Mar 12:11 This was from the Lord, it is marvelous in our eyes'?"

Mar 12:12 They tried to seize him, but they feared the multitude; for they perceived that he spoke the parable against them. They left him, and went away.

Mar 12:13 They sent some of the Pharisees and the Herodians to him, that they might trap him with words.

Mar 12:14 When they had come, they asked him, "Teacher, we know that you are honest, and don't defer to anyone; for you aren't partial to anyone, but truly teach the way of God. Is it lawful to pay taxes to Caesar, or not?

Mar 12:15 Shall we give, or shall we not give?" But he, knowing their hypocrisy, said to them, "Why do you test me? Bring me a denarius, that I may see it."

Mar 12:16 They brought it. He said to them, "Whose is this image and inscription?" They said to him, "Caesar's."

Mar 12:17 Jesus answered them, "Render to Caesar the things that are Caesar's, and to God the things that are God's." They marveled greatly at him.

Mar 12:18 There came to him Sadducees, who say that there is no resurrection. They asked him, saying,

Mar 12:19 "Teacher, Moses wrote to us, 'If a man's brother dies, and leaves a wife behind him, and leaves no children, that his brother should take his wife, and raise up offspring for his brother.'

Mar 12:20 There were seven brothers. The first took a wife, and dying left no offspring.

Mar 12:21 The second took her, and died, leaving no children behind him. The third likewise;

Mar 12:22 and the seven took her and left no children. Last of all the woman also died.

Mar 12:23 In the resurrection, when they rise, whose wife will she be of them? For the seven had her as a wife."

Mar 12:24 Jesus answered them, "Isn't this because you are mistaken, not knowing the Scriptures, nor the power of God?

Mar 12:25 For when they will rise from the dead, they neither marry, nor are given in marriage, but are like angels in heaven.

Mar 12:26 But about the dead, that they are raised; haven't you read in the book of Moses, about the Bush, how God spoke to him, saying, 'I am the God of Abraham, the God of Isaac, and the God of Jacob'?

Mar 12:27 He is not the God of the dead, but of the living. You are therefore badly mistaken."

Mar 12:28 One of the scribes came, and heard them questioning together. Knowing that he had answered them well, asked him, "Which commandment is the greatest of all?"

Mar 12:29 Jesus answered, "The greatest is, 'Hear, Israel, the Lord our God, the Lord is one:

Mar 12:30 you shall love the Lord your God with all your heart, and with all your soul, and with all your mind, and with all your strength.' This is the first commandment.

Mar 12:31 The second is like this, 'You shall love your neighbor as yourself.' There is no other commandment greater than these."

Mar 12:32 The scribe said to him, "Truly, teacher, you have said well that he is one, and there is none other but he,

Mar 12:33 and to love him with all the heart, and with all the understanding, with all the soul, and with all the strength, and to love his neighbor as himself, is more important than all whole burnt offerings and sacrifices."

Mar 12:34 When Jesus saw that he answered wisely, he said to him, "You are not far from God's Kingdom." No one dared ask him any question after that.

Mar 12:35 Jesus responded, as he taught in the temple, "How is it that the scribes say that the Christ is the son of David?

Mar 12:36 For David himself said in the Holy Spirit, 'The Lord said to my Lord, "Sit at my right hand, until I make your enemies the footstool of your feet."'

Mar 12:37 Therefore David himself calls him Lord, so how can he be his son?" The common people heard him gladly.

Mar 12:38 In his teaching he said to them, "Beware of the scribes, who like to walk in long robes, and to get greetings in the marketplaces,

Mar 12:39 and the best seats in the synagogues, and the best places at feasts:

Mar 12:40 those who devour widows' houses, and for a pretense make long prayers. These will receive greater condemnation."

Mar 12:41 Jesus sat down opposite the treasury, and saw how the multitude cast money into the treasury. Many who were rich cast in much.

Mar 12:42 A poor widow came, and she cast in two small brass coins, which equal a quadrans coin.

Mar 12:43 He called his disciples to himself, and said to them, "Most certainly I tell you, this poor widow gave more than all those who are giving into the treasury,

Mar 12:44 for they all gave out of their abundance, but she, out of her poverty, gave all that she had to live on."

Mar 13:1 As he went out of the temple, one of his disciples said to him, "Teacher, see what kind of stones and what kind of buildings!"

Mar 13:2 Jesus said to him, "Do you see these great buildings? There will not be left here one stone on another, which will not be thrown down."

Mar 13:3 As he sat on the Mount of Olives opposite the temple, Peter, James, John, and Andrew asked him privately,

Mar 13:4 "Tell us, when will these things be? What is the sign that these things are all about to be fulfilled?"

Mar 13:5 Jesus, answering, began to tell them, "Be careful that no one leads you astray.

Mar 13:6 For many will come in my name, saying, 'I am he!' and will lead many astray.

Mar 13:7 "When you hear of wars and rumors of wars, don't be troubled. For those must happen, but the end is not yet.

Mar 13:8 For nation will rise against nation, and kingdom against kingdom. There will be earthquakes in various places. There will be famines and troubles. These things are the beginning of birth pains.

Mar 13:9 But watch yourselves, for they will deliver you up to councils. You will be beaten in synagogues. You will stand before rulers and kings for my sake, for a testimony to them.

Mar 13:10 The Good News must first be preached to all the nations.

Mar 13:11 When they lead you away and deliver you up, don't be anxious beforehand, or premeditate what you will say, but say whatever will be given you in that hour. For it is not you who speak, but the Holy Spirit.

Mar 13:12 "Brother will deliver up brother to death, and the father his child. Children will rise up against parents, and cause them to be put to death.

Mar 13:13 You will be hated by all men for my name's sake, but he who endures to the end, the same will be saved.

Mar 13:14 But when you see the abomination of desolation, spoken of by Daniel the prophet, standing where it ought not (let the reader understand), then let those who are in Judea flee to the mountains,

Mar 13:15 and let him who is on the housetop not go down, nor enter in, to take anything out of his house.

Mar 13:16 Let him who is in the field not return back to take his cloak.

Mar 13:17 But woe to those who are with child and to those who nurse babies in those days!

Mar 13:18 Pray that your flight won't be in the winter.

Mar 13:19 For in those days there will be oppression, such as there has not been the like from the beginning of the creation which God created until now, and never will be.

Mar 13:20 Unless the Lord had shortened the days, no flesh would have been saved; but for the sake of the chosen ones, whom he picked out, he shortened the days.

Mar 13:21 Then if anyone tells you, 'Look, here is the Christ!' or, 'Look, there!' don't believe it.

Mar 13:22 For there will arise false christs and false prophets, and will show signs and wonders, that they may lead astray, if possible, even the chosen ones.

Mar 13:23 But you watch. "Behold, I have told you all things beforehand.

Mar 13:24 But in those days, after that oppression, the sun will be darkened, the moon will not give its light,

Mar 13:25 the stars will be falling from the sky, and the powers that are in the heavens will be shaken.

Mar 13:26 Then they will see the Son of Man coming in clouds with great power and glory.

Mar 13:27 Then he will send out his angels, and will gather together his chosen ones from the four winds, from the ends of the earth to the ends of the sky.

Mar 13:28 "Now from the fig tree, learn this parable. When the branch has now become tender, and produces its leaves, you know that the summer is near;

Mar 13:29 even so you also, when you see these things coming to pass, know that it is near, at the doors.

Mar 13:30 Most certainly I say to you, this generation will not pass away until all these things happen.

Mar 13:31 Heaven and earth will pass away, but my words will not pass away.

Mar 13:32 But of that day or that hour no one knows, not even the angels in heaven, nor the Son, but only the Father.

Mar 13:33 Watch, keep alert, and pray; for you don't know when the time is.

Mar 13:34 "It is like a man, traveling to another country, having left his house, and given authority to his servants, and to each one his work, and also commanded the doorkeeper to keep watch.

Mar 13:35 Watch therefore, for you don't know when the lord of the house is coming, whether at evening, or at midnight, or when the rooster crows, or in the morning;

Mar 13:36 lest coming suddenly he might find you sleeping.

Mar 13:37 What I tell you, I tell all: Watch."

I had to include all of these scriptures so you can see for yourself that there were no days ending or new days starting. Therefore, everything from Mar 11:20 to Mar 13:37 occurred on the 12th of Nisan. Now we come to the all-important verse Mar 14:1, here we are told the Passover is only two days away. If my maths are correct and I add two days to the 12th day of Nisan, I come to the 14th day of Nisan, the day Jesus was crucified according to the bible.

Mar 14:1 It was now two days before the feast of the Passover and the unleavened bread, and the chief priests and the scribes sought how they might seize him by deception, and kill him.

We started this countdown at the end of the day Jesus rode into Jerusalem on the 10th of Nisan, and after four days ended up on the 14th of Nisan. Therefore, the 10th of Nisan, when Jesus rode into Jerusalem was a Saturday and not a Sunday as traditional Christianity will tell you.

Therefore, if you are going to believe the word of God over the words of man. Palm Sunday is in reality Palm Saturday. Jesus entered Jerusalem on a Sabbath day.

Some people will object to this and say Jesus broke the law by travelling more than what is permitted on the Sabbath day. This is just another example of the traditions of man trying to replace the commands of God. Nowhere in the bible are we told about a Sabbath day journey, except when the teachers of the law make up their own rules and regulations.

This is the only way Jesus could have fulfilled the meaning of the day for selecting the lambs for the sacrifice.

FOOTNOTE.

Two commentaries in the bible differ in their views of days when Jesus rode into Jerusalem. If these so called experts on the bible can differ so much then we must go again to the only source of information we can rely upon as accurate. And that is the bible. Consider the following comments by Paul Kretzmann and F.B. Meyer.

PAUL KRETZMANN :- Mark here inserts a story of the Saturday before, when Jesus first came to Bethany from Jericho, unless we want to assume that two anointings took place.

F.B. MEYER :- This beautiful incident took place on the Tuesday evening of Passion Week,

These two bible commentators cannot agree on what day this happened, the first says it happened on a Saturday, and the second says it was on a Tuesday. so who is right? I have given you the evidence from the word of God, so why not just believe God, and not worry about the thoughts or traditions of mankind no matter how "expert" they may seem.

The Thief on the Cross

There is a great deal of important information we can learn from the episode about the two thieves who were crucified alongside Jesus. We do not know anything about these men except they were criminals sentenced to death because of their crimes. To find out what this occasion can reveal to us let us start in the book of Luke.

Luk 23:39 One of the criminals who hung there hurled insults at him: "Aren't you the Messiah? Save yourself and us!"

Luk 23:40 But the other criminal rebuked him. "Don't you fear God," he said, "since you are under the same sentence?

Luk 23:41 We are punished justly, for we are getting what our deeds deserve. But this man has done nothing wrong."

Luk 23:42 Then he said, "Jesus, remember me when you come into your kingdom."

This criminal may have heard of the miracles Jesus had performed but he was certainly not a follower of Jesus, he had but a few hours to live, and as we can see in verse 42 he asks Jesus to remember him when he comes into his kingdom. This thief is now professing he knows Jesus is his Messiah.

This thief is acknowledging Jesus as his Lord, therefore, he will be saved as is evident from the following scripture.

Act 2:21 And everyone who calls on the name of the Lord will be saved.'

The answer Jesus gave to this thief is very interesting, and it does provide us with a problem associated with the correct interpretation of this verse. First, let us read this answer in the NIV version of the bible to see how it was interpreted.

Luk 23:43 Jesus answered him, "Truly I tell you, today you will be with me in paradise."

The original scriptures were written in the Greek language, and they did not use commas. Therefore, the comma was placed in this verse in a position that best suited the original interpreters of the Greek. Some earlier books have the comma before the word today, while others put the comma after the word today. Consider the 2 versions of this verse below. One with the comma placed before today. Then consider the same verse with the comma after the word today, and see how it completely changes the meaning of the verse.

When you read the verse above with the comma before the word "today" it could mean that the thief and Jesus will both be in Paradise on that very day, the day they both died on the cross. But now look at that same verse with the comma after the word "today"

Luk 23:43 Jesus answered him, "Truly I tell you today, you will be with me in paradise."

Now Jesus is telling the thief today, that he will be in paradise with him, but this does not mean it will happen today; it will happen at some point in the future. We do not know how long in the future, so to find an answer to this, we must examine other scriptures that will shed light on this subject.

It is a very common belief today that when a person dies, they go straight to either heaven or hell. This false teaching will also be exposed in the rest of this chapter if you are prepared to accept the words of God over the teachings and traditions of man.

The Apostle Paul instructs us that we will all be resurrected from the dead. Please read carefully the following passage of scripture, it reveals the correct sequence of events that are to come.

1Co 15:20 But Christ has indeed been raised from the dead, the firstfruits of those who have fallen asleep.

1Co 15:21 For since death came through a man, the resurrection of the dead comes also through a man.

1Co 15:22 For as in Adam all die, so in Christ all will be made alive.

1Co 15:23 But each in turn: Christ, the firstfruits; then, when he comes, those who belong to him.

Jesus is the firstfruits of those who rise from the dead. If he is the first to rise then obviously no one has risen from the dead or gone to paradise before this time. Verse 22 tells us we will all be made alive or resurrected and this is followed by the all-important verse 23. Christ is the first to be resurrected from the dead, and the last part of this verse very clearly tells us it is when he comes, or returns, that the rest of the dead will be resurrected.

The 11th chapter of the book of Hebrews is called the "faith chapter". Here we can see some of the names of people from the Old Testament such as Abel, Noah, Abraham the father of the faithful, and Moses. Plus others who did mighty deeds in the name of God. So now let us examine from the evidence from the bible when these mighty men and women of God received their just rewards. The proof is in the following amazing passage of scripture that describes how they lived, and how they were treated.

These men and women all lived their lives by faith in God. Their lives are an example for us to follow today. Read the following to see how they were mistreated yet they never turned their backs on God, but they never received any of the promises God gave them, as we see in verse 39 and 40.

Heb 11:32 And what more shall I say? I do not have time to tell about Gideon, Barak, Samson and Jephthah, about David and Samuel and the prophets,

Heb 11:33 who through faith conquered kingdoms, administered justice, and gained what was promised; who shut the mouths of lions,

Heb 11:34 quenched the fury of the flames, and escaped the edge of the sword; whose weakness was turned to strength; and who became powerful in battle and routed foreign armies.

Heb 11:35 Women received back their dead, raised to life again. There were others who were tortured, refusing to be released so that they might gain an even better resurrection.

Heb 11:36 Some faced jeers and flogging, and even chains and imprisonment.

Heb 11:37 They were put to death by stoning; they were sawed in two; they were killed by the sword. They went about in sheepskins and goatskins, destitute, persecuted and mistreated—

Heb 11:38 the world was not worthy of them. They wandered in deserts and mountains, living in caves and in holes in the ground.

Heb 11:39 These were all commended for their faith, yet none of them received what had been promised,

Heb 11:40 since God had planned something better for us so that only together with us would they be made perfect.

All of these amazing men and women of God from the Old Testament have not received their rewards, as verse 39 clearly points out. They are all still waiting to be resurrected. Verse 40 then describes when they will get their rewards, and it will only be when the Apostles get their rewards,

Paul never comforted the living by telling them their deceased loved ones had gone to heaven. He always encouraged them by explaining the resurrection of the dead. Paul explains in the book of John that there will be a resurrection of both the good and the evil.

Joh 5:28 "Do not be amazed at this, for a time is coming when all who are in their graves will hear his voice

Joh 5:29 and come out—those who have done what is good will rise to live, and those who have done what is evil will rise to be condemned.

All those who are in their graves will hear his voice and come out of their graves. Martha, the brother of Lazarus whom Jesus raised from the dead was a friend of Jesus and had heard him speak often about the Kingdom of God. She knew and understood when the resurrection of the dead was to take place. Listen to their conversation in Joh 11:21-24.

Joh 11:21 "Lord," Martha said to Jesus, "if you had been here, my brother would not have died.

Joh 11:22 But I know that even now God will give you whatever you ask."

Joh 11:23 Jesus said to her, "Your brother will rise again."

Joh 11:24 Martha answered, "I know he will rise again in the resurrection at the last day."

When Jesus told Martha that her brother would rise again, Martha knew exactly what Jesus meant, and her comment in verse 24 is evidence that he will be resurrected at the last day and this is when Jesus will return in all power and glory at the end of this age. This thought is expounded upon in 1Th 4:15-18.

1Th 4:15 According to the Lord's word, we tell you that we who are still alive, who are left until the coming of the Lord, will certainly not precede those who have fallen asleep.

1Th 4:16 For the Lord himself will come down from heaven, with a loud command, with the voice of the archangel and with the trumpet call of God, and the dead in Christ will rise first.

1Th 4:17 After that, we who are still alive and are left will be caught up together with them in the clouds to meet the Lord in the air. And so we will be with the Lord forever.

1Th 4:18 Therefore encourage one another with these words.

Here in verse 16, it is very clear that the dead will rise when Jesus comes down from heaven. Those still alive will then ascend to the clouds to be with Jesus as well. Now look at the last verse. We are told to encourage each other with these words, and this is precisely what the Apostle Paul was doing. He was encouraging us to know the timing of the resurrection. How clear does he need to make this before people will believe the obvious truth?

OK, we got a little distracted from the thief on the cross story, so now we have established the timing of the resurrection when everyone will be resurrected, and that includes this thief. Let us continue in Joh 20:14–17.

This occurred when Mary went to the tomb to anoint Jesus but found the tomb empty. We know this happened on the first day of the week, Monday.

Joh 20:14 At this, she turned around and saw Jesus standing there, but she did not realize that it was Jesus.

Joh 20:15 He asked her, "Woman, why are you crying? Who is it you are looking for?" Thinking he was the gardener, she said, "Sir, if you have carried him away, tell me where you have put him, and I will get him."

Joh 20:16 Jesus said to her, "Mary." She turned toward him and cried out in Aramaic, "Rabboni!" (which means "Teacher").

Joh 20:17 Jesus said, "Do not hold on to me, for I have not yet ascended to the Father. Go instead to my brothers and tell them, 'I am ascending to my Father and your Father, to my God and your God.'"

This happened at the empty tomb, and the most vital point to understand here is in the last verse. Jesus tells Mary not to hold onto him because he has not yet ascended to his Father. Do you get the point of this? Jesus was in the tomb for three days and three nights; he rose from the dead late on the Sabbath, but here, early on Sunday, he has not yet ascended to his Father.

Since Jesus had not ascended to his Father until Sunday, then how could the thief on the cross have ascended to paradise on the day they both died on the cross? The comma was definitely in the wrong place. The only plausible explanation is that the comma was in the incorrect place in Luk 23:43. When the comma comes after the word today, it all makes perfect sense. Jesus told the thief he would one day be in paradise, and this would be at the same time all other believers in Jesus would enter paradise. On the last day, as Martha correctly understood.

There will be people who do not accept that a villain like this thief could enter paradise after only confessing Jesus as his lord with only an hour or two left to live. Let me explain why they are wrong, and as long as you believe in Jesus as your saviour, it does not matter when you come to believe; as long as you believe, Read Act 2:21 again.

Act 2:21 And everyone who calls on the name of the Lord will be saved.'

And if this is not enough proof for you then please read the parable Jesus told his disciples in Mat 20:1:16.

Mat 20:1 "For the kingdom of heaven is like a landowner who went out early in the morning to hire workers for his vineyard.

Mat 20:2 He agreed to pay them a denarius for the day and sent them into his vineyard.

Mat 20:3 "About nine in the morning he went out and saw others standing in the marketplace doing nothing.

Mat 20:4 He told them, 'You also go and work in my vineyard, and I will pay you whatever is right.'

Mat 20:5 So they went. "He went out again about noon and about three in the afternoon and did the same thing.

Mat 20:6 About five in the afternoon he went out and found still others standing around. He asked them, 'Why have you been standing here all day long doing nothing?'

Mat 20:7 "'Because no one has hired us,' they answered. "He said to them, 'You also go and work in my vineyard.'

Mat 20:8 "When evening came, the owner of the vineyard said to his foreman, 'Call the workers and pay them their wages, beginning with the last ones hired and going on to the first.'

Mat 20:9 "The workers who were hired about five in the afternoon came and each received a denarius.

Mat 20:10 So when those came who were hired first, they expected to receive more. But each one of them also received a denarius.

Mat 20:11 When they received it, they began to grumble against the landowner.

Mat 20:12 'These who were hired last worked only one hour,' they said, 'and you have made them equal to us who have borne the burden of the work and the heat of the day.'

Mat 20:13 "But he answered one of them, 'I am not being unfair to you, friend. Didn't you agree to work for a denarius?

Mat 20:14 Take your pay and go. I want to give the one who was hired last the same as I gave you.

Mat 20:15 Don't I have the right to do what I want with my own money? Or are you envious because I am generous?'

Mat 20:16 "So the last will be first, and the first will be last."

When it was time to pay the workers, he wanted to give them all an equal wage. This upset those who had worked the entire day, as they believed they deserved more than just one denarius. However, the landowner reminded them that they had agreed to work for a denarius when they began early in the day, so they should not be upset if he paid those who worked for a shorter amount of time the same amount.

The same principle applies to those who come to Jesus late in life. Jesus desires to reward us with eternal life in his kingdom. Faith in the Son of God is crucial, as it is what will ultimately save us. Good deeds alone will not suffice for salvation; only faith can accomplish that. Like the thief on the cross, our rewards will not be realised until Jesus comes again.

Let me explain it now from my point of view. I have had faith in Jesus for many years and hope to enter his kingdom some time in the future. Why should I feel hard-pressed if someone turns to God in the last hours of their lives? Surely I should be exceedingly happy that they have found that faith and will end up in God's kingdom. It is my job to spread the gospel to everyone, the young and the old. If I felt the elderly who came to faith late in life did not deserve to be admitted into God's kingdom, then I should only preach the Kingdom of God to the young who can spend a lifetime in faith. I hope you can see the futility of that thought!

The First Fruits

The feast of first fruits is another day that the vast majority of people do not understand, but it has a great deal of meaning to those who have searched the scriptures and found the truth God has concealed in his holy bible.

The feast of first fruits is given to the Israelites in Lev 23:9-11.

Lev 23:9 The LORD said to Moses,

Lev 23:10 "Speak to the Israelites and say to them: 'When you enter the land I am going to give you and you reap its harvest, bring to the priest a sheaf of the first grain you harvest.

Lev 23:11 He is to wave the sheaf before the LORD so it will be accepted on your behalf; the priest is to wave it on the day after the Sabbath.

Let us establish firstly when this particular day unfolds. The Passover is held on the 14th of Nisan and this is followed immediately by the Feast of Unleavened Bread, which starts on the 15th day of Nisan and runs for seven days.

Lev 23:6 On the fifteenth day of that month the LORD's Festival of Unleavened Bread begins; for seven days you must eat bread made without yeast.

Lev 23:7 On the first day hold a sacred assembly and do no regular work.

Lev 23:8 For seven days present a food offering to the LORD. And on the seventh day hold a sacred assembly and do no regular work.'"

Four days after the Passover on Wednesday the 14th of Nisan we come to the day after the weekly Sabbath. This is the day God ordained the Feast of firstfruits to be celebrated.

I find it interesting that Palm Saturday was four days before the Passover, and now we see the Festival of Firstfruits happening four days after Passover.

There was a very special event that happened four days after the Passover when Jesus was crucified. We have established the fact Jesus was resurrected from the tomb on the Sabbath. The women went to the tomb early on the first day of the week, that is Sunday, only to find the tomb empty.

Joh 20:1 Early on the first day of the week, while it was still dark, Mary Magdalene went to the tomb and saw that the stone had been removed from the entrance.

Joh 20:2 So she came running to Simon Peter and the other disciple, the one Jesus loved, and said, "They have taken the Lord out of the tomb, and we don't know where they have put him!"

Now skip to verse 11 and read to verse 18.

Joh 20:11 Now Mary stood outside the tomb crying. As she wept, she bent over to look into the tomb

Joh 20:12 and saw two angels in white, seated where Jesus' body had been, one at the head and the other at the foot.

Joh 20:13 They asked her, "Woman, why are you crying?" "They have taken my Lord away," she said, "and I don't know where they have put him."

Joh 20:14 At this, she turned around and saw Jesus standing there, but she did not realize that it was Jesus.

Joh 20:15 He asked her, "Woman, why are you crying? Who is it you are looking for?" Thinking he was the gardener, she said, "Sir, if you have carried him away, tell me where you have put him, and I will get him."

Joh 20:16 Jesus said to her, "Mary." She turned toward him and cried out in Aramaic, "Rabboni!" (which means "Teacher").

Joh 20:17 Jesus said, "Do not hold on to me, for I have not yet ascended to the Father. Go instead to my brothers and tell them, 'I am ascending to my Father and your Father, to my God and your God.'"

Joh 20:18 Mary Magdalene went to the disciples with the news: "I have seen the Lord!" And she told them that he had said these things to her.

What happened on this first day of the week? The tomb was found to be empty and the body of Jesus was not there. Then Jesus appears to Mary and she recognises him. One very important aspect of the first meeting between Mary and Jesus is found in verse 17. Jesus tells Mary not to touch him because he has not ascended to his Father, and then he says to her to go and tell his brothers he is going to ascend to his Father. Mary could not touch Jesus at this time because he had not ascended to his Father.

After this encounter with Mary, Jesus then appeared to his disciples as described in Joh 20:19.

Joh 20:19 On the evening of that first day of the week, when the disciples were together, with the doors locked for fear of the Jewish leaders, Jesus came and stood among them and said, "Peace be with you!"

We are told again this all happened on the first day of the week. This is obviously a very important point to establish if we are to fully understand what happened on that day. The book of Luke gives us the next piece of vital information. Now Jesus is with his disciples in the upper room and he is assuring them he is real and not a ghost.

Luk 24:38 He said to them, "Why are you troubled, and why do doubts rise in your minds?

Luk 24:39 Look at my hands and my feet. It is I myself! Touch me and see; a ghost does not have flesh and bones, as you see I have."

What is so important about these verses? First, remember that Jesus told Mary not to touch him because he had not ascended to his Father, but now, in verse 39, he instructs the disciples to touch him. This can only mean that sometime between seeing Mary at the tomb, and then appearing to the disciples, he did return to his Father and then came back.

This chapter has been written to help you understand the meaning of the term "firstfruits." The very name of this feast implies thanksgiving to God for the firstfruits of the annual springtime harvest. The Israelites offered the very first sheaf of the harvest to God and were not permitted to eat of this harvest until this first sheaf of the crop was offered to God.

We were shown from the word of God that this day is to be celebrated on the day after the Sabbath following the Passover, as instructed in Lev 23:11. This is the same day Jesus ascended to his Father, as the above scriptures have shown.

So this first sheaf of the crop offered to God represents Jesus coming before his Father after he had risen from the dead the day before on the weekly Sabbath.

This is why Jesus is often called the firstfruits in the New Testament. Paul explicitly explains to us Jesus fulfilled the Feast of Firstfruits by being the first to rise from the dead, and that everyone else who has ever died will also be raised from the dead, as the following verses advise us from the book of 1 Corinthians 15:20–23.

1Co 15:20 But Christ has indeed been raised from the dead, the firstfruits of those who have fallen asleep.

1Co 15:21 For since death came through a man, the resurrection of the dead comes also through a man.

1Co 15:22 For as in Adam all die, so in Christ all will be made alive.

1Co 15:23 But each in turn: Christ, the firstfruits; then, when he comes, those who belong to him.

When Jesus rose from the dead, he was the first to do this and that is why he is referred to as the firstfruits. Then in verse 23, we are assured we will also be raised from the dead, but each in his own turn. Jesus was first and when he returns we will have our own resurrections from the dead.

2 Th 2:13 and Jas 1:18 reinforce these clear teachings from the bile.

2Th 2:13 But we ought always to thank God for you, brothers and sisters loved by the Lord, because God chose you as firstfruits to be saved through the sanctifying work of the Spirit and through belief in the truth.

Jas 1:18 He chose to give us birth through the word of truth, that we might be a kind of firstfruits of all he created.

The bible is a most remarkable book and when you look for clues about who the real author is, you will find proof in many areas that cannot be explained away apart from someone with foreknowledge of what is going to happen. In the Old Testament, we see a perfect example of this. Read Job 19:25-27 below to see how Job understood there would be a resurrection from the dead.

Job 19:25 I know that my redeemer lives, and that in the end he will stand on the earth.

Job 19:26 And after my skin has been destroyed, yet in my flesh I will see God;

Job 19:27 I myself will see him with my own eyes—I, and not another. How my heart yearns within me!

The Feast of Firstfruits is the day Jesus ascended to his Father. He is the fulfilment of this feast. As I stated in the introduction of this book, Jesus did everything "by the book" to fulfil every prophesy about himself.

Conclusion

The title of this book is "The Purpose of Jesus The Christ". So now we have a little more knowledge of him we must decide what the purpose was for him to come to the earth, to suffer, and be crucified on a Roman cross.

The short answer is he came to bring salvation to us all, to be able to share eternal life with him in his kingdom in a place of perfect peace and where evil cannot exist. A place so opposite to the one we all live in here on this earth. No more sadness, no more tears or crying, Just a time of joy.

Anyone can enjoy this type of a future but only if they are prepared to obey God and to live by what he expects from us. If we do this we are guaranteed a place in his kingdom, but if we refuse to accept Jesus Christ as our Lord and Saviour, then we are going to the other place and I am sure you will know what I mean.

When we die there are only two places we will end up. Either we will be in God's paradise or we will be in the fires of Hell and you are the master of your own destiny. The Roman Catholics will tell you of a third placed called purgatory where you can eventually buy your way into Heaven, The only trouble with this idea is it is found nowhere in the bible. In fact if you diligently search the scriptures you will find this is indeed a false teaching, a heresy. Consider the following verse from the book of Romans.

Rom 6:23 For the wages of sin is death, but the free gift of God is eternal life in Christ Jesus our Lord.

Here we have a choice, death or eternal life. There is no third option.

Eph 2:8 for by grace you have been saved through faith, and that not of yourselves; it is the gift of God,

Eph 2:9 not of works, that no one would boast.

Another thing to consider is found in the above verses. Life is a free gift from God because of our faith and trust in our Lord and Saviour Jesus Christ. There is no amount of good works that we can do that will get us into the kingdom. Why is that? The answer is in verse 9, that no one can boast.

Let me explain. If two men die, one very wealthy who has done a lot of good things with his money, and the second is a very poor man who barely survives on his wages. If God looked at the good works we do, then the rich man will be rewarded much more than the poor man, even though the poor man may be more devoted to God, who lives according to the laws of God. Whereas the rich man may be doing all his good works to seek the praises of his fellow man and not so much to please God. This is why God says "that no one can boast".

Our inclusion in God's paradise comes only from our faith in Jesus Christ. This makes the playing field level for the rich and the poor man. Both will be judged not by what they do, but by the devotion to their Lord Jesus Christ. Please consider also the following verse.

Rom 3:23 for all have sinned, and fall short of the glory of God;

Everyone sins, and the only way we can be cleansed from our sins is by accepting Jesus Christ as our Lord. There is no other way and that includes doing good works. So now the question is "Why do we do good works?". The answer to that is simply because we now understand we are already saved through the sacrifice of Jesus Christ, so we want to do our good works as a way of thanking him for what he has already done for us. Good works can never be a way to buy your way into the paradise of God.

Yes, we have all sinned and wandered away from God, but Jesus is our good shepherd and all of our sins were laid on him when he died on the cross. If we are prepared to accept the blood he shed for us, then we are guaranteed a place in God's kingdom.

Isa 53:6 All we like sheep have gone astray. Everyone has turned to his own way; and Yahweh has laid on him the iniquity of us all.

Therefore, Jesus came to this earth to bring us all salvation if we will just accept him, and that is the point, we must accept him. We must cultivate a personal relationship with him through the daily study of the bible and daily prayers.

There is no substitute. To just say you believe in Jesus and do nothing to build that all important relationship with him, then you are falling short of the mark and risking your place in God's kingdom.

Where does God fit into all this. He is a perfect and holy God who cannot abide with sin. He never wants to punish us so he made a way for us to escape his punishment for our sins. He did this is the most loving way he could. He allowed his son Jesus Christ to be crucified on a roman cross in our place. We all deserve the death penalty. but Jesus has paid for our sins but only if we accept his sacrifice.

The most important thing we must do is to remember the sacrifice Jesus made on our behalves, remember the blood he shed, and the pain he endured all for our sake, that we may be free from the penalty of sin. He has purchased a place for us in the Kingdom of God which we claim only by trusting in Jesus and keeping our faith in him strong.

About The Author

Leslie Rendell worked most of his life in an agricultural support industry, mostly in the supply of spare parts for machinery. Since his retirement in 2014 he has dedicated much of his time to bible study and writing books as he comes to understand biblical topics.

He understands the bible is a very complex book and one that is easy to misinterpret and believes this is one of the main reasons why there are so many different version of the bible and different religions around the world.

What he writes is his own interpretation of God's holy scriptures. He studies the thoughts of other writers to try to see things from their point of view, but always comes back to the bible as the final authority on any topic. His main aim in writing, is to give anyone who is seeking the truth from God's words a starting point in their own research.

Leslie's other interest are photography, and his growing family.

Don't miss out!

Visit the website below and you can sign up to receive emails whenever Leslie Rendell publishes a new book. There's no charge and no obligation.

https://books2read.com/r/B-A-VDUV-ENDHD

BOOKS 2 READ

Connecting independent readers to independent writers.

Also by Leslie Rendell

Bible Studies
Three Days and Three Nights
According To Your Faith
Do Not Conform
How Long Was Jesus Christ in the Tomb
The Law of Moses
Abraham, Jesus and the Cross
Do We Have Immortal Souls
Be Holy
Is Being Fearful A Sin Against God
Mockers and the Return of Jesus Christ
Teachers During The Tribulation
Tearing of The Curtain in The Temple
The Thief On The Cross Alongside Jesus Christ
What Is The Rapture
The Imminence of the Rapture is a False Teaching.
Why The Pre-Tribulation Rapture Theory Is False
Are You Hindered By Satan
Satan is Targeting Man's Free Will
Why Is There So Much Suffering In Our World
The Sign of Jonah
Evil Is The Rejection Of God
Satan, Spirit Being With Many Names
Have Faith In God
Only One Sign
The Lord's Passover

The Resurrection of Jesus Christ
Jesus The Christ
The Purpose of Jesus The Christ

Watch for more at https://www.leslierendell.com.